Soul Searching

Soul Searching

Rajkumar Mukherjee

PARTRIDGE

To order additional copies of this book, contact
Toll Free 800 101 2657 (Singapore)
Toll Free 1 800 81 7340 (Malaysia)
orders.singapore@partridgepublishing.com

www.partridgepublishing.com/singapore

Contents

My Epitaph

Here lies the heart and soul of a poet
Who searched true love all through life;
World laughed at him, lovers ignored—
Let new generations find strength in strife.

About the Author

Born in an upper middle-class family with great honor and respect for traditional values, Rajkumar did his post-graduation in commerce from University of Calcutta. After retiring as a banker, he went back to his first childhood love, poetry. His poems were published in School and College magazines, local journals and even overseas journals namely, "Prism" at regular intervals. During his college and university days, he edited and published number of literary journals from Calcutta and Purnea, India.

His first book of poems was published from Calcutta in 1975. In 1980, he edited an anthology of poems on Tagore with contributions of eminent poets of Bengal and Bangladesh. In 2009, two of his books were published from Calcutta. One was a translation of Maurice Carême's book, 'Songs of Beginning' from French to Bengali.

This is a book of poems by Rajkumar mainly on nature, love, spirituality and philosophy chosen and published during last five years. He is a regular contributor to www.poemhunter.com, www.mypoetryforum.com and www.allpoetry.com. His poems are regularly published in Prism international, magazines, IPF anthologies and Ink Angels, printed anthologies of the allpoetry.com.

Dedication

To my wife Sipra
My   son   Pratik
Daughter-in-law Shilpa
My daughter Ragini
And Son-in-law
Debashis

Author's Note

"Soul Searching" is an unending journey. The seeds of searching were sown in my mind long back during sacred thread ceremony when I was just thirteen years old.

Slowly over the years, the journey took shape through my youth, through turbulent twenties, theatrical thirties, fairy forties. But the fifties and sixties found its pinnacle and mind settled on its goals. The last two decades, perhaps, was for assimilating the ideas and touching on experiences of life... Sad and sombre, bad and breathtaking, good and gorgeous, ethereal and eternity, political and perversion, but all are percolated through the experience of life.

So the poet in me, cried at the sordid affairs of the society, sympathizes with the people living below the poverty line, took part in the protest march against any kind of oppression in any part of the world, massacres of peace loving people by any individual or group in the name of religion or whatsoever.

Simultaneously it rejoices at blooming of a new flower in the flower pot in my balcony, the fragrance of jasmines brought by south winds in the evening or staring at the smile of a child in the park opposite my house.

This is a collection of some of my award winning writings during last five years published in different magazines, journals and online, mainly through AllPoetry.com, International Poetry Fellowship, Poem Hunter.com, My Poetry Forum and of course, Prism.

My thanks to my friends in All Poetry to mention a few, Brother Dennis, Ron Wiseman, Andre Emmanuel Bendavi Ben-YEHU, Rolinston and Jo Ellie. My thanks to my son, Pratik Mukherjee, but for whose help and active participation, the book might not have seen the day of light.

If someone somewhere can relate to the feelings expressed in my book that will be a prize for me. Any constructive criticism of the poems and the book as a whole will be highly appreciated.

August 15, 2016
Singapore

Foreword

''Soul Searching ''

The book ''Soul Searching '' by Poet Rajkumar Mukherjee brings a universal poetic voice to readers around the globe — delivering a bouquet of mixed flowers — with fragrances of wisdom; scent of awareness of the beauty of life; and its multiple visions of social strata.

''Soul Searching '' is a depiction of the journey of a Soul that saw the beauty and the ugliness of the actions of Man; — a Soul that sought to understand humanity; and to secure a course of harmonious growth — and understanding. It is the vision and emotion of a son that tried to do his home work; of a father that learned to grow with the children; and a grandfather that wants to course on the path of peace, and edifying life.

The readers of all ages will find the contents of the book, "Soul Searching" to be a jewel for the treasure of the mind and the Soul.

Much gratitude to Poet Rajkumar Mukherjee for adding value to the literary treasure and for enriching the history of Poetry.

Gratefully,

Andre Emmanuel Bendavi ben-YEHU
New York City, NY. August 28, 2016

Foreword

In his book "Soul Searching", Author Rajkumar Mukherjee poetically explores life, love and the daily interactions with whatever crosses his path with a thoughtful caring heart that tempers his writing that endears us as readers. His humble and wise spirit armed with his mastery of poetic expression share his seasoned perspective in a friendly, readable format. You'll be drawn by his passion and compassion and will seek more of his diverse and profoundly beautiful poetry.

I have known Mr. Mukherjee for a number of years and know he is sincere and his integrity is most admirable and you will witness that reflected in his work. I, without any hesitation endorse this author and this book and have every confidence that you will be blessed by reading "Soul Searching" by Rajkumar Mukherjee.

Thank you,

Dennis L. White
Poet and Author
Carleton, Michigan. August 27, 2016

Futile Fury

The bull inside me
wish to change,
snake wants to bite,
the storm within
creates a tempest,
wailing waves
break their heads on sands.

Even the full moon fails
to quieten my nerves,
hands are tighten,
can't change
the state of affairs,
mind tortures heart
in futile fury.

Peace-Haven

In my dreams, I win millions,
live in mansions gorgeous,
drive a red color Ferrari,
wear watches precious.

Though I live in a hutment
with a thatched roof on top,
my heart and mind stay on stirrup
but no money to shop.

If I had some spare in my purse,
perhaps, I would have dreams
of peace in this world of ours,
generations won't scream.

Empty stomach never holds dreams
of prosperity, peace,
bereft of hate and greed of others,
river of life brings bliss.

In Line With "Splash" by Charles Bukowski

the mirage is
you are
listening to this tune,
in reality the tune is
much more,
it's a song,
an evening Raga
Yaman Kalyan
played on Sarod,
a mid-night raga
Mallkus
played on Sitar,
Ashavari
played in morning
in a flute or violin
dwindling between
hopes and despair
resembling your pain;

this is Tagore
singing aloud
in your heart,
Nazrul speaking
for unification
of two Bengals,
calling loud
for revolution;
the tabla
in rapid fingers
of Alla Rakha
creating the sound
of marching soldiers
on horse back
with open bayonets:

it is Bukowski
visiting a brothel
to know their pain
first hand
and stunned to find
a lover of his poems
who can share a night
gratis
in exchange for
a poem, a true picture of life;

the tiger roars
in the Sunder-bans
crocodile tears are shed
in the banks of
the Ganges, the Brahmaputra,
the Satlej and the Kaveri
the Brahmins alone
with meticulous perception
pronounce the slokas
mixing all waters together
but the minds, the hearts
of millions rotate
in different directions
bringing bloodshed
in the name of
language, religion;

yet day turns to evening
evening to night
with the promise of
another golden morning
when we know not
whether we will see it
or at least our
next generation.

Points To Ponder (Baba Style)

Who do you wish to partner life,
a charming lady, or household wife,
a dancing partner in social strife!

A lady with lot of wealth behind,
for common man she will be unkind;
your sickness too, she might not mind.

Love might be a matter of laugh,
going along might become tough,
yet in your home, she fits like dove.

Who do you wish to live in with
in down-to-earth life, or in myth,
dreams die fast, as balloons reach plinth.

Haibun-Museum (Tanka Prose)

Who knew, a visit to the museum in my city will bring in ancient Egypt before my eyes! A mummy of a Pharaoh from the Pyramid land is lying in the big hall. But alas! No photography is allowed.

I just sat there for a while and it seems that he is speaking to me carrying the desert storm through the oasis. But I failed to realize and relocate to the memory of the Pharaoh. Was he ever guarded by the Great Sphinx or Giza?

what you guard Giza
knowledge kingdom Sun-God
desert sands know
knows the river Nile
blowing storm across

In Line With Sharon Olds

Sometimes, I feel hounded by my predecessors
for not doing anything that was expected of me,
hardly I can answer them
in midnight dreams,
I panic in sweating, choked throat,
toss and turn in bed for rest of the night.

Sometimes, I fight questions by you, my wife
from distant stars, I don't have any answer,
you warned me ahead of time
but with youthful vigor
I overlooked all of them,
as a result, I'm suffering today.

Sometimes, I face questions from you, my son
about my failures,
indifferent attitude to family,
and work alcoholic nature, a servant of 24/7 hours,
as a result, I have nothing
to leave for children, wife
they too are suffering with me for my faults alone.

These unborn questions, poems,
stories of gone by years haunt my nights,
allegations taunt my existence,
they are lost in dreams
leaving me lonely in a vacuum;
however I try, I can't find
syllables, words, imagery, metaphor
to give shape to those unborn lives.

Haibun—April Storm

Small clouds in shape of a vulture gather in north-western corner of the sky. Like a political gathering, one by one they arrive and forms a skyline that suddenly erupts as a storm and covers the canopy of sky soon. The impact of the storm felt by coconut and other long trees first. Some of them are uprooted. Rivers are in spate and so does the sea. Tornado hits the coastal line. Fishermen's coves are gutted. High-flying birds hurry back to earth only to find some of their nests are nowhere.

Quickly follows the rain. Bare-chested children make most of it, they dance like peacocks to welcome the first rain of the season.

on kites' wings

storm invades earth

rain-dance begins

Je Suis De Paris, Aujourd'hui.

Today, my heart belongs to Paris,
a city of culture, arts and poetry,
my heart roams in air, along the Seine,
boulevards, lanes and Gothic lines.

My heart belongs to you today
city of Bastille and Montmartre,
I smell gun-powder, paint picture
of scattered limbs within theater.

I belong to you damsel, this hour
when cowardice paints blood-stains
on your pavements, laments of mother,
wife and children, fill up sky in vain.

Today, my heart belongs to Paris
birthplace of Liberty and Equality;
I know, tomorrow will be another day,
Renaissance will bloom paintings, poetry.

World will cry for a week or two,
voices will rise against dastardly acts,
but the days are not far when you'll show
how to finish terror, tear them apart.

Sleep oh lady, sleep in pious peace,
carrying with you, all the bliss,
new generations will learn from you,
love's true meaning, Parisian beau.

Vignettes In Line With Rumi

I
Lost in trifling issues
I squandered my life;
never known when you came,
knocked on my door,
and left unceremoniously;
"crying" has no value any more.

II
Between you and me
an ocean of tears
accumulated over the years;
joy and pain, love and loss,
all are mingled together for eternity;
who can change course of destiny?
neither you nor me.

III
Now I'm traversing this celestial ocean,
stars, planets, keep me company
in my search for a new route to Heaven;
I pass by the black-hole of death, a cemetery,
carrying with me your love,
no tears, no fears, no sorrows,
for an everlasting tomorrow.

Death, My Love

Tip-toes you're closing in
to snatch my heart from body
like a prowling tiger;

like a rattle snake
charming me with your sweet melody,
removing my pains, agony.

I can visualize the Milky Way
with my closed eyes
opening before me--
next course of journey.

Who knew you're so beautiful!

Rendezvous

Eyes meet eyes
lips on lips
T
H
R
O
B
B
I
N
G

sensation
S
D   P
N   L
A   A
H   y
TOUCH

game continues
till outburst in

U
N
I
S
O
N

ECSTACY

Self-Realization

I opened my eyes
mesmerized with your beauty
lost verbose
with love and longing
realized reasons, raptures
judgement close

loss lingers pain
I tried to change
social stigma

I was such a fool
changes I sought for
were for me alone
now I know
you were right
I took uncalled for pride

now I try to adjust
with you beautiful earth
you made me wise.

Inspired by "Rollins Sailboats"
by Charles Dickinson

River knows the story of banks
floating clouds, of blue sky.
Man in the middle knows the depth
of mackerels, where to try.

Little speed boats wait their turn
when the drizzles start,
flocks of fish will start bite on baits
however they are smart.

I sit by the river alone,
lost in no thoughts prime.
Across the river blows the bells,
creating evening chimes.

Life and love mingled together
in this serene moment,
birth and death hide below water,
everything is God-sent.

Memorial Day Prayer

Let me extend my shoulder
and carry your casket to the grave
at least for a day, let us be brave
and go beyond barriers of no-man's-land;

you too be gracious
in accepting my flowers, chrysanthemums,
lotus for the last rites;

let sky overflow
with incense sticks of jasmines
in place of toxic gun-powder,
let our voices mingle today
in a joint prayer.

The cold kiss of death
has touched our forehead...
both yours and mine,
you might have lost your brother,
me, my husband,
my son, his father,
are we not sailing in the same boat?

Let's join hands
in carrying caskets containing cadavers
to the mass grave,
it might lighten our grief
and add value to prayer for peace,
for next generation;

let's pronounce together--
OM SHANTI!
OM SHANTI!!
OM SHANTI!!!

Resolution On Valentines' Day

we will not build
a castle of hope
in the sky
rather we live a life
fraught with poverty
strife
still never shy
to announce
our everlasting love
for each other
like a nestled dove...

Love Songs Cry

emotions run high
in midnight rain
umbrella fly

when love comes pouring
in Boulevard Seine
who can deny

love wins love
night to remember
Parisian damsel

in one corner
rose bouquet fumble
love songs cry

Gathering Dust

Your glossy cover invites me
quickly I turn pages,
white and blue lining turns me on
dig out words from ages.

In moonlit night your face aglow
with love, passion divine;
fossilized syllables come alive
as if took bath in shrine.

You come to me in birthday robe
asking for graffiti,
my pen sketches your face alive
words of praise in poetry.

Day after day in lonely hours
our love story blooms,
years pass and hidden records
you hold in your blossom.

Few of them finds place in a book,
some a place in journal,
mostly they gather dust in corner
though holds love eternal.

Season—Cinquain

I

Autumn
in shifting mood
sheds her leaves for rabbits
winter takes over, disrobes her
Spring blooms.

II

Love is
held in close heart
blooms with warmth of lover,
beloved knows forthcoming change
ageing.

Rainbow Teachings

At land's end,
the cross glows with blessings of lord;
villagers, fishermen got delighted.

Rainbow holds all colors within,
irrespective of caste, creed, religion,
what more one can ask for?

Reflection on the creek, speaks volume
about His last costume,
jeweled with nails, envy of society.

Rainbow shows us direction to Heaven,
expands our horizon,
love, compassion and sobriety.

Love-Songs Written On Parchment

Floating maple leaves brought on shore,
parchment of poetic, love adore,
symbol of love held code galore.

What lay hidden on leaves' content,
wondrous symphony, lone hearts' song;
lovers stayed apart, some restraint
kept them away, from where belong.

What was written on those parchment,
best love poems of lovers' time spent;
first time we saw it, though not meant.

There was a Knight and his own lass,
spent together days and lone nights;
history of love written on sash,
swords pierced through them in moonlight.

Broken Dreams

Broken dreams like shards,
pieces of glasses
fly as splinters,
all over my head.

Broken words like floating clouds
vacillate alone in cerulean sky,
I can't hold them in my net
however hard I try.

Broken love like unfulfilled desire
holding truth behind will,
infatuated--
yet I could feel.

Broken dreams fly like parachutes,
like wisteria and cotton seeds,
sow lives far and near;
they take away my youth, my time,
but instill new life
in this forest, called society;
I repent, yet take pride in it.

Beyond The Fence

Beyond the barbed wire
lies hope, freedom, light,
let's go, hold hands tight.
Homeland, we're leaving
for the sake of generation,
no arguments, commotion.

Some of us crossed sea
to reach Europe in time,
a few lost their life prime.

I can hear cry of Aylan Kurdi,
'Papa, please don't die,'
on sand, seagulls feel shy.

Humanity lost its charm,
barbarians control, harm,
infected ISIS germ.
If alive, we can build again,
thrive with hope, not despair,
God's blessings, let's share.

Little Angel

Caterpillar to butterfly
a journey towards beauty
nobody can deny.

Humans try to imitate
with utter failure;

mosaic colors on wings
create magic tapestry;

beauty of flowers are glorified
by your fluttering fantasy.

Little Angel,
you're God's marvel of creation.

Wings Have Limits

A child learns everything
by keen observation, touch and taste,
he learns to differentiate
between good and bad,
safe and danger, through experience;

he depends mostly on his mother.

Once we rely solely on Mother Nature,
gather experience
through success and failure,
we will learn our limits, our capabilities,
without any hangover of ego, pride,
any God-like all powerful feelings.

We will know how to swim
across a turbulent river,
between birth and death, called life;

then there is no turning back
for us, the mankind.

Confucius To Tiananmen

Dragons fly in my dreams,
opium no more beyond Chinese Wall,
Red Book, I adored once
only next to Lenin;
Communism left its burnt,
Tiananmen Square, still haunts my mind.

Economic super-power leaves her sleep,
growing curves steep
mesmerize the world body;

yet the time has its twists and turns,
curves are mischievous, burns
with ups and downs;
exports plunge, brings devaluation,
some term it as manipulation.

Rich culture flows unabated
withstanding the tamed yellow river,
literature and spirituality shines bright
to light dark corners of humanity.

Wish you come back soon, in full flow
ignited by the philosophy of
Confucius, Lao Tsu and the Buddha.

Life To Afterlife

Theory of negation is fine
liked by pessimists,
yet life has its glorious days,
fear and fight persists.

Who can deny fragrance of rose
and reach her without thorns,
yet we, humans fight within,
throughout night till morn.

This life is just a cog in wheel
other cogs are ahead,
we don't have choice to break away
till reach our floral bed.

Negation leads to affirmation
to reach ephemeral life;
let's try hard, assimilate all--
enjoy life in its strife.

Love's Language (For A Lady In Love)

How could I know so many languages
to convey my feelings only for you,
but the young lass, with charming eyes,
I do care and I'm in love with you.

When our eyes meet, the universe know,
pounding heart holds, mind hides the glow,
trembling lips, clog the vocabulary,
cryptic message, decipher finery.

Without saying a word, you say so much,
my eyes lower in accepting and hatch
new dreams for future, together we'll sow,
in Garden of Paradise with love's glow.

Our love-story written in signs and braille,
it's the strongest, without any frail,
my poems show, sketches glow your face
care and love, nobody could deface.

Recluse

When you hide into your cell
like a snail,
in dusky gloomy shadows,
all my efforts fail
to enlighten you
settle our disputes.

I wish to bring cheers,
bright up your light-less heart,
but uncompromising you
stay apart.
Moonless night is filled with
shriek of owls,
nocturnal creatures
delve deep into earth.

Occasional rhapsody of nightingales
glisten up your eyes,
but it's not enough
to brighten our night;
I find recluse in my somber heart.

Unto Him

Rely on Him
when in danger,
when you suffer
from loss of confidence.

Rely on Him
when in joy, happiness,
share with Him-
your joy re-doubles.

Rely on Him
as He is the only savior,
will stand by you-
in hours of distress.

Rely on Him
a l w a y s
as you came from Him
and will mingle into
after bodily death.

Hyacinth—Unrequited Love

Even Gods are not beyond jealousy,
they have their hidden lusts, twists and turns,
Zephyr killed Hyacinth by playful run,
Apollo was in deep love with youth's beauty.

She did not allow Hades to touch his body,
turned him into a beautiful flower;
even today lovers share, sympathy,
enjoy its fragrance and varied colors.

Gods fight like us for supremacy--
but flowers in heart still blooms intimacy.

City of Joy

Silent protesters light up night,
unity music holds them tight,
unique love-story burns up bright.

Slowly moves procession by inch,
cars stand aside, though feel a pinch,
love binds together without hitch.

City has seen protesters' march,
be it in Winter or in March,
history is known to Gothic arch.

Phosphorous—Trijan Refrain

I came to beach in search of pearls,
waves wash my feet with sands;
I lift my skirt, remarked sea-gulls,
'take care of your pink hands';
waves run over galloping heart,
blue sky drives, boat of clouds apart,
waves run over-
waves run over-
love floods in my billowing heart.

I came to beach in search of pearls,
never knew where they hide;
time passes by, nothing unfurls,
within sands, bush behind,
I feel alone, in wide wide beach,
lone company keeps, cold sea breeze;
I feel alone-
I feel alone-
how far are you, I pray, beseech.

I came to beach in search of pearls,
who lay hidden in heart;
how can we be together, snarl
up, the distance apart,
I drown in love, like nesting dove,
hush-words lie hidden in alcove;
I drown in love-
I drown in love-
like phosphorous it blinks, true love.

Independence Day

Independence day I know from sky
When evening sets in on 4th of July,
Stars bloom in different colors,
Canopy of sky comes down near;
In joyous mood people dance, sing--
What a scene together they bring.
Fire crackers boom and rockets fly,
To usher in a new dawn none deny--
Flower balls fly encircled garlands,
On sky dais-- new beguiles bands,
Lincoln Washington's pictures float--
All through the night in sky's boat.

At last for a day the strife's forgotten,
Political economic wars left open,
People make merry of their own.

They Wrote In Blood

They suffered death every moment,
tortured within prison cell;
they knew outside
their families, neighbors were suffering,
yet they stood united in chains.

They wrote, "Freedom"
with their blood on prison wall.

Let My Words Speak

Let my words gallop
like Arabian horses,
to fight against all oppression
anywhere in the Globe,
in the name of economic chain,
or bondage of supremacy.

Let my words garner strength
from faith and beliefs,
gain speed of wind and light,
to fight anarchy, injustice,
and bring peace
among humanity.

Let my words cross over seven seas,
mountains, ridges, cliffs,
to reach the heart of the needy,
the poor, insignificant of society,
and even out the disparity of wealth.

Symphony—Monotetra

She pours her heart out, moonlit night,
keeping her hidden, from our sight,
calls out for mate, with sweet delight,
at dead of night, at dead of night.

Her mate has gone for distant tree,
failed to return, before sun free--
and travel to south to bring glee,
no joy to flee, no joy to flee.

Her songs bring joy and lone hearts bloom,
the budding buds in nature's loom,
earth and sky floods in joyous zoom,
their nest it's gloom, their nest it's gloom.

Cuckoo's songs bring moon's symphony,
stars join in with trumpet's agony,
wind blows music--love's destiny,
I feel lonely...I feel lonely.

Inspire

Your words inspire me,
motivate me to excel,
eradicate all weaknesses
kindle my spirit in heart.

Your songs cajole me
in lone hours of night,
provide solace in sorrows.

Your paintings prompt me,
stimulate my senses,
ignite my imagination again.

You smile through framed dark glasses.

Shadow Acrostic—April Fool-Life

Allegiance turned to Allegation,
Paucity, privacy to Publicity,
Reliance changed to Relegation,
Independence to Interdependence;
Longing and lust to Love.

Flowers yet bloom, Flourish
Originality to Origami;
Oceans of Omnipresence,
Life finds eternal Love.

Teacher

1.
snail crawls up
to taste young leaves-
birds of prey prowl

2.
love digs deep in heart
wavering indignation-
root cause of cancer

3.
banyan tree stands
withstanding gale and storm-
family comes first

4.
nature is great teacher--only if we learn

Source-Code

I lift my eyes to sky
search for you, like a sky-lark,
but you are not found anywhere;

I look around the forest
greenery, flowers pacify my mind,
fruits--my hunger,
but my hunger for you remain un-satiated;
I stroll on the river on my boat,
enjoy the ripples, their songs,
I feel your touch with wet winds;

I lift my eyes to hills,
where you dawn upon daily,
energize us to task till dusk
to begin a day anew.

I know and realize
your presence,
you are the source,
you are the beginning-
and end of life.

Silence

snow on snow --silence
paratroopers drop in
quietness prevails

rocking chair swings
you left for cemetery
never to return

in silence
love speaks louder
do you listen

You

You carry memories of my lover
in your fluttering wings;

You bring velvety touch
of her lips on my cheeks;

You dress up like a bride
as was she on her wedding night;

You mesmerize me with your beauty,
butterfly.

Alas!

Wind blows in all directions,
never comes back with change of seasons
rivers flow continuously,
water of high-tide never returns in low-ebb;

Sun-shine and moon-light appear to be same
but depicts different pictures in mind;

lost childhood, youth under pressure,
wish I could re-visit,
re-start afresh,
mend all mistakes, lost opportunities.

But alas! no one has time
to stop by and listen
to my childish appeal.

Love Alone

Love came and gone,
when---never known;

time tickles by.

Now I know,
I can't hold her back,
yet wrap my hands
around her,
in futile revenge.

OM...

Let my prayers transcend-
from troposphere to exosphere,
your lotus feet;
let it bring
your blessings--
my meditation
for mankind.

Let Love Warm Hearts

No more snow please,
enough is enough,
I'm drowned to my neck,
epitaph has lost its name.

We wish to breath fresh air from south,
spring flower,
cherry blossom,

Let's bid farewell to mist and fog,
no more logs in fire-place,

Let love warm our hearts.

Human Bondage

She got rid of the clutches of Octopus,
they robbed her chastity,
clothes and left her in the woods;
exhausted--
she lay bare and naked,
yet dreams of white roses
bereft of thorns and shackles.

Humans left jungle to animals
and built society,
to protect, prosper and ensure safety.
Now it is infested by animals
with human masks,
no more safe for loners.

Yet she dreams of peace,
white roses, doves,
quietly sleeping in warmth of fire
left by them, the infiltrators
of her privacy, to protect her
from the gnaws of wild animals.

Solidarity

Volatile hearts --yet expressionless face :

cowardice overpowers peace-loving citizens,
they never voice protests;

disregard oppression, economic or otherwise-
as if never seen or heard.

Peace of cemetery now prevails the world over,
fear psychosis keep us mum;

yet when someone ignites the voice,
pen sketches, writes poetry or plays,
structure a sculpture of unchained labor,

flood waters sip into souls,
we unite, wear black badges,
hold processions in the name of solidarity.

New Beginning

Quietude prevails,
silence prolongs-
peace converts angst;

differences die down,
harmony of souls
boil down to love;

from edge of divorce-
new beginning.

You Are My Soul-Mate

Search ends--
soul finds soul-mate,
through years of longing
weeping river
meets sea.

Till youth--
I'm waiting for you,
unison of earth and moon,
epitome of love--
universe watching tonight.

Let My Words Speak

Let my words gallop
like Arabian horses,
to fight against all oppression
anywhere in the Globe,
in the name of economic chain,
or bondage of supremacy.

Let my words garner strength
from faith and beliefs,
gain speed of wind and light,
to fight anarchy, injustice,
and bring peace
among humanity.

Let my words cross over seven seas,
Mountains, ridges, cliffs,
to reach the heart of the needy,
the poor, insignificant of society,
and even out the disparity of wealth.

We, The Commoners

Shades of oak, lengthen
with setting sun,
dark clouds bring
early evening ;

hovering jets indicate,
shape of things to come
during night;

in insomniac dreams,
shadow of war
cover my eyes,
like wings of vultures;

somewhere--
some war-lords
celebrate victory,
on the backdrop of
loss of innocent lives.

Forever Glow

'There are those who feel the pull'
of earth's gravity and nectar cool;
flowing river and blowing wind,
rising ocean and cooling mind.

There are people who feel the urge,
beautify nature with color splurge,
add music to rivers, bird-song,
poetic bells chime a ding dong.

There are few who cry for others,
in their bad times, in lonely hours;
that's why earth is still in motion--
love endures life's commotion.

Let river of life forever flow--
sun and moon in sky ever glow.

Last Words

Like any other day
evening folds his wings
behind the mango grove;

visiting hours are over,
security staff blow their whistle
for visitors to leave;

your last words
'Will you take me home tomorrow?'

that night never dawned
a day for you,
the last words
still haunt me-
in my lone hours, mother!

Festival of Lights—Vignettes

I
Your eyes glitter in joy,
win over demons produce
dance of light over darkness;
wearing garland of slain heads
you forgot Shiva lying below.

II
Ignorance is deepest darkness,
you light candles of knowledge;
yet gloom persist
in the eyes of on-lookers,
humanity torn apart.

III
Win of good over evil
will it come at all,
why then Ebola, ISIS,
why ghosts of World War III--
loom large in horizon?

IV
Hope shattered in fears,
voice of protest choked in despair;
Oh Mother, rise again,
destroy demons among us and within,
greed, hate, and unhealthy passion,
bloom love-light, hopes luminous.

Forty Words On Lips

Like a firefly it mows
the grasses in dark,
like phosphorus it glows
leaves it's spark,
attracts me to your
parted lips.

Lips dance on lips,
heart pounces on heart,
the untold story of love
is sketched under starlit sky.

ABC of Life—Vignette

I
To know Atman is a tall order
yet we must strive for him,
soul-searching is the only path,
don't count on life, it may be lost;
still if you could touch His feet,
departure lounge --there is no grief.

II
Since birth you have taken all,
natural gifts, air, water, food,
beauty of flowers, Sun and Moon,
bird-songs, clouds and monsoon;
have you given anything in return,
it's time to be benevolent, you.

III
Without commitment what is life,
vacillating goals vitiated by strife
half-hearted attempt gets half-result,
never ever reach full throttle;
commit you must to know thyself,
thus you reach His Lotus feet.

View-Point

Prolongation of pain in pensive hours,
hidden under the skin
below the rib-cage,
punishes his patience.

Still he lingers smile on his face,
not to bother others,
paints his feelings
on parchment with pen;

persistent protracted pain
brings ultimate peace.

I Wonder

Life prolongs--
gathering air in lungs,
vision in eye-lashes,
dreams in heart;

When the heart ails,
land turns to desert,
blessings of rain dries up:

Where from you gather strength,
my soul,
how you turn your leaves green,
beautify garden?

Close To Heart—Vignettes

I
Love came close last night,
full moon created magic,
east wind brought rains,
jasmines made air heavy;

II
You were not around,
tears formed rivulets,
cuckoo's calls remain unanswered,
nostalgia sips in heart :

III
porous sip-page breaks plinth,
mind vacillate,
determination falters--
ageing steps in;

IV
Science and art fights,
quiet hours of night
pierced by owl's hoot,
yet love blooms with new sun,
life and trust prolongs.

Pathway

The pathway leads to never-land
where love holds hands of sun and sand;
beautiful birds sing songs of hope,
hatred, jealousy find no scope.

Segregated trunk --still he stands,
shows us the way to never-land;
we come, visit, joyous return--
never bother for tree's heart-burn.

Only birds know story of pains,
wind brings solace in breeze and rains.

Love Is...

&

love is a dove
flies in clear blue sky
lighted by sun-rays

&

love is butterfly
flies from flower to flower
collects nectar --rainy-days

&

love is crimson rose
opens petals to lovers
thorns to invaders

&

love is a flower
once smelt-- no use for worship
decorates your hair

&

love's red liqueur flows
as milk for children –nectar
satiate my thirsty lips

Abject Surrender

When sky surrendered to cloud-bursts,
hills submitted to snow, blizzard, avalanches,
tempest flooded the coastal-lines,
earthquake created havoc all around,
Tsunami leveled the 'haves' and 'have-nots';
I left my pride aside
and surrender to you, my Lord.

Looking Back

Project life I approached with gusto,
enthusiasm knew no bounds;
decades passed--
childhood to youth,
youth to married life,
mass movement to poetic.
your nearness added flavors to love:

Lost zing in everything now,
await your cold hands, my beloved.

Illuminated

I saw glimpses of your face
covered in dupatta,
glances of your eyes;

My days are dark now–
nights illuminated.

Limitless Sky

You are like a chameleon,
change your colors
throughout days and night,
through seasons,
in my eyes, mood,
hopes, despair, expectations.

They say, "Sky is the limit",
no, you are not,-- limitless sky,
first rays of sun
sown dreams within.

Anticipation—Contrary Thoughts

Buds wished to bloom as flowers,
flowers to fruits,
youth forgotten--
reached ripe old age.

Love flowed quietly
all these years,
in search of beloved.

You await beside my bed
in anticipation--
preparing for next journey,
ultimate re-union of soul-mates.

Forgiveness Is Love

It's time to leave love for love's sake
enshrine eternity--
in memories of living take
held in serenity;
love is pious, love is golden,
knows no age bar, gets embolden,
love is pious
love is pious
blooms as lotus, in heart's garden.

We lived a life in stress and strife
withstood envious eyes,
shared happiness, turbulent life,
without a vile or vice;
love is gorgeous, love is sunshine,
love stands tall as an erect pine;
love is gorgeous
love is gorgeous
without love, nothing is fine.

You stood by me and me with you,
in love's tests at all times,
love won battles in all but few
where serpents held in chimes;
love is forgive, forget all faults,
quiet in heart love does install,
love is forgive
love is forgive
in my epitaph, let it scroll.

Ascendancy

Sky is overcast:
darkness hovers in day-time
like moment of death of Ashwathama
in the Mahabharata;

Values deteriorate,
scams take upper-hand,
rowdiness, piracy prolong;

yet I know--
at the end
goodness will prevail over evils;

ascendancy of mankind
is certain.

Nature Prevails

life is futile
if it cannot light candle
in dark corners

cannot bring smiles
on faces of depressed
food to needy

why am I alive
just to regenerate
and die

I hate such life
I'll prevail
leave marks on society

Silhouette

lone tree standing at the cliff
enjoy touch of the sea
happy to be in his warm embrace
she knows well his love
is destined to bring her end one day
like it did to so many others

small forestry has lost its glory
over the years
still love-waters sip in slowly
to her roots
for ultimate re-union

only silhouette and nesting birds
know her story

Fishy Love-Affair

I had a doubt
about her dubious nature,
vacant look,
occasional strange behavior;

one day the can opened with cry,
piscine smell
of clandestine affair surfaced;

she still loves me--
but spends time with her brother
a cancer patient.

Justice

They say, 'Justice delayed is justice denied.'
in their preamble to law books
but never delivers, never follows;

dithering process
fills pockets of advocates
peshkars and amlas--
year after years

scam-filled society
adds to pocket-money
under the table;
dates change hands

Judges changed with new Government
faith in democracy gets a boost

thinkers become passive
surrender to apathy
inaction of large scale.

Mystique Philosopher

Inquisitive eyes
searching for prey in darkness
yet humorous appearance
hoots the night
with shrill shouts

Shakespeare found it
"a merry note"
marvel of nocturnal creatures

beautiful yet cruel
merciless
when hungry

my companion of most nights
in village home
by river-side
mystique philosopher

Meditation

suspended pendulum
swaying from right to left,
toss of the coin-
head or tail;

suspended animation
holds truth in hushed voice,
diplomatic disclosures of doctors -
increase anxieties;

behind the scene, hiding
you watch in cool anticipation,
smile at the ignorance of humans;

quietly I move to
my meditation room.

Destiny

Solitude sucks,
crowded place abominable,
loose talks
leave me bore;

in quiet protest
I recoil--
in my cell.

Life outside moves on--
to certain destiny.

Light

you breathed life unto me
I became alive
aware of good and evil
unaware of how to deal with

You read my mind, hesitation,
torn off the haze, the mist
with your light

my notions are clear now
mission of life known
route demarcated

your throne glistens
at the end of tunnel
wish I could reach
till I breathe last

The Buddha Speaks

(Buddhang Saranang Gachhami)
(Sanghang Saranang Gachhami)
(Dhammang Saranang Gachhami)

His eyes are closed
deep in meditation
searching
analyzing knowledge
for finding perfect remedy
for human beings

His lips are shut
quiet
choosing
toying
with the right words
to utter when time is ripe

He is smiling
forgiving
pardoning
all our foolishness
eagerness
to come to premature conclusions

He pronounces three words
forgive
love
search

He demarcates the path
faith
religion
togetherness

the bells ring in peace
monks travel through earth
our world becomes a better living place

Last Journey

cobweb of mist
torn by sun-shine,
eternal light
illuminates last journey:

carried on Angel's wings-
ethereal music of stars
covers dying moments;

dazzling milky way,
darkness of Black Hole,
shatters vision;

yet end of tunnel-
your glowing abode beckons me.

Love & Life—Joseph's Star

Love
blooms like a
Lotus, in life's pond
cajoled by bees and south wind
holds dew on petals awhile
till the scorching sun
evaporates for
good

****

Life
encircles
off-springs and neighbors
drunk in Maya's servitude
like bees in pond of nectar
till your call arrives
eternal
soul

Tribute To A Great Soul
Mother-Poet Maya Angelou

Through your eyes--
we visualized our freedom,
in your words--
we found consonance of our cherished dreams,
in your memoirs--
our childhood brightened, memoirist -poet,
promises of youth
cemented with determination and grit;
you had been so close to our heart
we could never differentiate
your dreams with ours;
your absence Mother-poet,
has created a vacuum--
that can never be filled by any;

we take new oath today
to follow your path,
fight for our rights,
sympathize with suffering masses,
carry them towards your mission of life.

Vignette—Ebb

I
withering leaves fly
across nebulous sky
tempest follows
raindrops bring solace
skylarks reach to greet

II
failure to ensure
economic revival
die away hopes
of young generation

III
flowers desiccate away
in hot summer
yet dreams flourish
in clear cerulean sky

Tagore After One Hundred Fifty Years

You dreamt of a young poet
reading aloud your poems
in shrouded darkness of evening

Let me admit
even after a century and a half
I cannot think of any expressions
of joy, sorrow, happiness
beyond your poems and songs

You have covered us like a canopy
a sky with varied colors beyond which
we can never send our dreams
the law of gravitation brings us back to ground

City of joy enjoys her
morning, evening, night
with your songs playing around
in every street-corners

Are you not making us crippled, lethargic
like the old villagers
opiated with your poems, songs and dramas
which are so amazingly true
even after a lapse of hundred and fifty years

Angel's Highway

the winding road
through virtuous greens
holding tapestry of shade and sun

the canopy of branches' leaves
shelter birds bees
humans alike

the guard of honor by trees
taken by Angels
at the end of tunnel--Nature's way
awaits God.

Lily

I'm Calla lily--
blooming alone in summer wind,
raising my eyes to sun;

nectar of love flows--
drips from my petal's edge,
glorifying the morning;

bees gather, so do photographers,
lovers, morning walkers,
mesmerized they stand;

I smile to them--
unaware of alluring white beauty,
just for a couple of days.

Diagnosis

Love bloomed when and how we knew not,
Cherry Blossoms can't withstand breeze,
petals flew aground on green grass
stitched tapestry of pink carpet.

we could diagnose it only through
lowering of your eyes, thumping of my heart,
craving to meet, longing, strong desire
that burns our body
even if we are momentarily away.

Let's submit to wishes of God
I confess my love for you forever.
Will you...?

Why?

there is a silent sigh
passing through night-sky
questioning the God 'why' 'why'

sagely hills and soulful rivers
join in the flowing murmurs
lonely forests nod 'nay'

blooming flowers in quiet pots
think for a while whom to nod
decide to commit their 'aye'

yet we humans fail to learn
continue to kill and burn
our fellow brothers, never shy...

Where Lies The End of This Journey?

where lies the end of this journey
called life, death is end of a tourney,
but river flows on to ocean,
evaporation, formation of cloud,
again rains bring them back;

what next, where do meet
all these love, desire, hate?

'Silence S'il Vous Plait'

Perhaps there was pain,
yet the joy overwhelmed--
collage of colors unbound;

graffiti in sky--
soothed her mind and ailing soul
ventured for eternity;

perhaps there was thought,
for children others behind--
moonlit patio garden bloom:

green yellow and red,
overshadowed by white--
as if in a Milky Way;

'silence s'il vous plait',
no more lights and fire-crackers-
she is asleep in harmony;

jasmines strewn in bed,
stars blink her path to Heaven--
blowing breeze pacify pain.

Hide-Out

find fault with others
anyone can without harm

when searching within--

Pandora's box opens up
hidden desires pop out

Time Waits

with ageing
attack of writers' block increases
whatever I write is pedestrian
muse takes a back seat
dastardly hours pass by
no ink flows from my quill
back home
I search within
nothing is lost
elegant ancient civilization
left hidden underground
awaiting your arrival
future generation
I bow to thee...

Ethereal Voice

jasmines swing their heads
in evening spring wind,
river's murmur join chorus of stars;

alone in garden my heart breaks,
no cracking sound fills thin air--
wailing... sobbing... in ether.

Awakening

light particles vacillate, flicker
like insects against light,
rising sun plays the trick quietly all around me,
I feel existence of life,
illuminated souls abound,
efforts to analyze fails with reasons--scientific, social;

I look at the vast sky, listen to the wind,
passing through trees and murmuring river,
and realize why
cooperation and tolerance are the essence of peace;

I fall back to your Lotus feet
to know self and the ion of lights
surrounding me like fire-flies at night,

You simply smile at my ignorance...

Unfathomable

river of life flows on--
how many bridges I build
between you and me,
love, hate,
language, religion, society?

gaps widen
like horizon, sky,
oasis in desert,
your love---

unfathomable...

Trust

New born's reliance on mother,
wingless bird's belief in trees, sky,
never verify, never shy--
unconditional surrender
to you alone is trust.

Give me the faith and belief
acquired from previous birth;
let me swim like a fish,
in troubled waters of earth,
to return to you unhurt.

Old Is Gold

Old flames never die, stay quiet
underneath the heart like a hearth
waits the moment for air to flash
old flames never die...

old habits die hard, flourish again
when you make a new friend
with similar habits and liking
old flames never die...

old loves never die, awaits call
from the beloved, voice plays trick
touches the heart, fires up love again
old flames never die...

old songs never die, churn the heart
with old tunes, soul joins the party
invigorates the ethereal love within
old flames never die...

old poems never die, live in memory
of the lover and beloved inaudibly,
touch of five senses heralds again
old flames never die...

old desires never die, sprout like
seeds with the advent of Spring
rain-drops bring serene smiles
old flames never die...

Oh God Why!

blast over-powered visitors
blood-stained bodies float as cadavers
vultures hover around sky
only witness the big clock
captured precise time of blast
lonely survivor stands
mesmerized-- frightened
shouts, 'Oh God why!'
howling wind passes by...

Treaties On Love

crystallized dew drops
accumulate in heart--
transformed by soul as diamond;

constellation of stars add light,
full moon's glamour---glitterati,
cuckoos swing in melodious rhythm;

soul-mate acts as catalyst,
unites long lost friends
across seven seas hills and lives:

mind adds speed of thought
wind the fragrance touch-
dream brings taste vision,
forgiveness soothes souls;

quietly a flower blooms
in the Garden of Eden
enlightens earth and heaven;

night after night
you collect meteorites
and give shape to dream fruit;

a sudden burst in solar system,
human dynamics--fall of apple
brings Adam and Eve together--
love flows forever... thereafter;

Heaven transformed to Earth.

Words

my lens is clicking
sky is raining words
you hold in your palms
dripping

my lens is storing
falling snow on pines
shining sun
diluting

a child is crying
no shed no food
helpless mother
begging

words are slipping
failing memory
unable to hold them
depleting

closing my eyes
is the only solution
before my birthday
pleading

Fruition

Ideas lie frozen under the carpet of snow
like the green grass of Autumn
now barren, colorless...at best brown.

resolutions take back seat,
immediate demands prioritize,
manuscripts gather dust in one corner.

yet I know, like the blooming shoot of a grass-
with the advent of Spring, suddenly the lawn will sprout
with blooming poems, printings of heart.

then one evening you and me together-
spend the night under candle light and give shape to the
symphony
with glittering graphics to adore the page of poesy.

ideas and resolutions
will reach their desired fruition in abundance.

You bloom alone
bursting through rock of rapids
colorful bonanza;

butterflies die
for your beauty, nectar,
wild wind whispers
gossips of love,
spreads fragrance;

moonlight stores
history of creation,
Nature's bounty
once in a couple of years...

Union Of Soul Mates—Loop Poem

Senses propel experience,
experience brings feelings,
feelings come through touch--
touch, see, hear, taste, smell.

Smell turns on our mind,
mind dreams of union,
union with the soul mate,
soul mate hears our call.

Call of the wild in the forest,
forest carries whispers of wind,
wind and water cannot cool,
cool the desire burning within.

Within we long to touch,
touch and taste forbidden fruit,
fruit created through communion--
communion with the God.

God's bless comes with meditation,
meditation whispering in river,
river holds hidden story of love,
love practiced by sages through ages.

Ohne Poetic

Without a poetic vision
Artistic touch, you're mere doll;
Love would have pass you by, wind shy
Touch your hair, without emotion.

Unless they saw beyond surface,
Without a poetic vision,
Philosophical vibes, notion,
Mona Lisa would have no grace.

Love would have been just ritual
Without lust, feelings sensual,
Without a poetic vision--
Life would be devoid of passion.

Artists, poets and philosophers
Made our life, book of art and verse;
Reality would stand aside--
Without a poetic vision.

I Know Not When She Will Call

(Reverse Nonet Double)

So I kept my doors ajar with hope
that she will return before grave
call me finally to arms
neighbors pour handful dust
over my coffin
last glass of wine
sipped slowly
complete
rite

ஃ

last
never
lasts forever
soul finds new form
womb, foster mother,
from dust to kingdom flows
river of love, ---unhindered
greatness, love of the Creator
eternal love story of you and me

Welcome

backdrop of blue sky
lilies swing their heads—welcome
anchoring signal
Proposal

A bridge to cover
between life and death
between love and hate
between Earth and outer Universe

feelings and emotions
placid quietude and wild horse
present and past
starlit nights and moon-beams
golden sunshine
pitch-dark black hole

will you join hands with me
in my sojourn
to know the unknown
magical wisdom
ethical virtues
promise to cross the bridge
the river that divides
you and me
till we reach unison

I Love You My Baby

I love your innocent smile
intimidating style
vision on life and vile

I love your eye-lashes
flying French kisses
word that hisses
my ear never misses

I love you as it is
with or without bliss
forever long for your kiss

I love you my baby
in your entirety...

Hands of God

When I see no shadow of yours beside me
I feel deserted, when I need you most;
what a fool I am!
In the desert sand, you held me on your palms
to guard against heat and dehydration,
condensed the rain drops to quench my thirst,
cool the sand for me to walk back to the oasis.
Should I ever forget your kindness, oh Lord!

Love Poem In Parchment

Your words are sharper than snippets,
yet I appreciate love they beget,
behind the jharoka eyes search--
muslin dupatta pride demurs;
quiet in heart love flower blooms,
in garden I reach for poem's parch,
sharpened bamboo-shoot turns to pen-
with blood I write eternal pain;
hidden hope that once you will see,
true love story encrypted plea,
lovers' paradise this garden--
cherish ever by men-women;
all lovers seldom reach their goal---
lives through lives entwined heart and soul.

She Awaits

She dwells within-- all alone
with her fears, disbelieves,
but a firm expectation
that one day he will come back;

neighbors know he will not,
he has gone to the land
from where nobody returns,
she is disgusted with their behavior--
their crocodile tears;

she fears the night for its darkness,
shadows, ghostly appearance,
she likes moon, jasmines
and crimson roses,
store-house of memories
of their last meeting;

she knows they laugh at her
for her belief on that is non-existent,
fear for the darkness,
her hallucinations, paranoia;

neighbors still admire
her love for the person she was in love with
but who is no more.

Love's Bless—Monotetra

You and I together will sow--
Seeds of love that will ever glow,
In moonlit night with river's flow--
We took a vow, we took a vow.

Wind carried that solemn declare,
Removed sorrows and all despair;
Hearts filled with joy that dare to bare
Our love and care, our love and care.

Time passes by with warmth and chill,
Old owl hooted at night with shrill;
Indicating of change -time's drill
Our baby they kill, our baby they kill.

Now we cannot see face to face,
Love has fallen from lofty grace;
We blame each other for this mess,
Love yet bring bless, love yet bring bless.

Cross-Roads of Life

You left me stranded in cross-roads of life,
I know not which way to go further;
life is strewn with sufferings and strife—
rose petals are dried, thorns lay scatter.

Promises galore, vows undertaken—
Lies buried in heart like seeds in womb;
When hopes are shattered, life forsaken,
I stare at my future in catacomb.

Where goes the days of glitter and light,
Poetical soiree, musical charm?
Whose envious look brings us this blight—
Once an ideal couple, think of harm.

Oh God! You know how summer brings rain,
Can't you bring back my lover again?

Ecstasy

eyes on your eyes
sky opens up like rose-petals

inviting tender lips quiver
sends signals of unspoken love

heart-throbbing hardens nipples
your caressing increase flow of adrenaline

I close my eyes like a foolish hare
your arms binds us together

doe could not speed away
makes ultimate surrender
lips on lips -- we entwine
doves reach ecstasy in unison

Love –Triolet

Our love is pure and held us bold,
Trees stand witness—serene affair-
In summer spring or chilling cold,
Our love is pure and held us bold.
Wind spreads stories of love untold,
Young souls hint of hope and despair-
Our love is pure and held us bold,
Trees stand witness---serene affair.

Young souls hint of hope and despair--
We remember our days of gold,
Past brings smell of your jasmine hair,
Young souls hint of hope and despair.
Time has taken toll, free and fair--
Yet love strengthened quite embold,
Young souls hint of hope and despair--
We remember our days of gold.

Garland Cinquain—Love Wins

My love
stays afar
beside river Rhine
in a small town by Black Forest
alone

she waits
meditates
in lonely hours
to achieve the eternal
quiet

her love
flourished in hills
at the Himalayas
whilst we were together searching
for peace

our paths
changed direction
in our youthful glamour
when and why nobody knows for sure
love cries

afar
we stay-- yet close
soul-mates meet in quiet
ethereal web-link in dead night
love wins

My love
meditates
at the Himalayas
when and where nobody knows
love wins

Your Touch

Your touch makes me shiver
eyes drop down to earth
cheeks blush with crimson red
knees tremble like aspen leaves
somewhere down a river flows

your scent makes me mad
long to hold you hard
rose petals open quietly
invites bee to pollinate

your deep blue eyes
provoke me to plunge
and swim in your vastness

lips on lips you sow seeds of dreams
in my heart and soul
I never wish to return
from that day-dreaming feelings

I feel reborn in your
touch smell taste and vision
I hear the songs of our last life
and togetherness
I can never forget and cherish forever

A Wish-List

No more tears, no more oppression
of female by male-dominated society,
no decease and death due to starvation,
no waste of food, no malnutrition.

Distribution of wealth almost equally-
liberty to all, education, medication,
lead me the way two thousand thirteen-
and breathe fresh air, I will bow to thee.

Rondeau On A Beach

Love me dear, in this forlorn beach,
Moon alone lights this dark peach,
Your eyes closed in expectation--
I am lost in your smell, deep blue ocean,
The pounding of heart wants to reach.

Fear me not; I am your true lover,
Shall be with you always forever;
Let me kiss your eyes and lips,
Love me dear.

love me dear and hold me close,
Let's bare each other and enclose;
Only the moon will stand witness,
To our love making! I confess--
Never to leave you in duress,
Love me dear.

Lost Trust—Cross Sonnet

In love we lost our life's prime time,
who knew there was true love sublime?
where body not count, priest or ghost,
our life's prime time, in love we lost.

The man you trust betrayed you ever,
neither loved children, nor even care;
alone you managed, as you must,
betrayed you ever, the man you trust.

Money you earned, spent on gamble,
wine, whine, women where dolls tumble;
now sick in bed, like charcoal burned,
spent on gamble, money you earned.

I know you can't regain lost trust,
God forgive you, pray to Him last.

Sleep—Rondeau

I cannot sleep, because I dream,
they drop at midnight, I scream;
all my predecessors and friends-
ask why I tolerate misdeeds?
I don't have answers in my dreams.

I don't have peace because I think
of my neighbors, blue, green and pink,
I share their agony and distress--
I cannot sleep.

I don't have joy because of love,
In sky they fly like pair of dove;
observe sorrows like Happy Prince,
who cannot say anything but mince,
surrender gold for poor's love;
I cannot sleep.

World Smiles Back

You smile to the world
world smiles back,
saying "Hello" does not cost you anything--
the smile you get back makes your day.

Love flows from one heart to other
'Wingless bird'—eyes reflect notion;

Before judging others,
why not judge yourself,
have you done your home-work-- to stay afloat?
In this world of conflicts and care,
pains and share,
love and smile pervades all senses.

Time Never Stops, Chimes Do.

I have an image of you my mother
the kitchen is so calm---
no stirring of spoons to dilute sugar
no addition of milk and cream.

Before I wake up half of household
works were finished
including your lunch box and mine;

Only the wall clock at main hall
chimes its pendulum at regular interval,
reminds me of your last days--
resembling your heart beat though uneven;
and the moment of passing away
when the other clock stopped permanently...

The Troika of Creation

(MAMEKANG SMARANANG BRAJO
Based on the Geeta chapter 10, Sloka-25)

Among the great sages
of all ages
I am Bhrigu
who could see three worlds
visualize in three dimensions
past present and future of the creation

Among words of communication
I am the prime sound
that holds all in OM
the single letter
when pronounced correctly
can bring solace to mankind
from pains, disease, sadness and sins

Within all pujas and rituals you perform
to appease Gods and Goddesses
I am the prayer without which
you can never reach them

Among all immovable objects of nature what
apparently are stagnant at the same place
for years together, I am the Himalayas
who through his own meditation
can bring back rain-clouds
develop forests vegetation
and melt the ice on its peak
in such proportion to maintain
rivers lakes fountains and seas
adequately fed all the time

Believe in me Arjuna, I am the creator
the preserver and the destroyer
the Troika of creation
birth life death all are fixed by me
so why do you bother yourself
for killing your kith and kin
in this religious war
whose fate is already written
in my own hands.

```
77
7777
777777
7777777
777777777
777777777
7777777
777777
7777
77
```

Significant Seven

Why seven
neither three
nor five nine eleven
seven oceans on our earth
seven seas-seven colors of rainbow
discovered by Sir Isaac Newton
seven rounds to take a vow
seven wonders of world
ancient and present
seven heavens of
Islamic tradition
seven dwarfs
in the fairy tale
seven days of a week
seven day story of creation
seven chakras of meditation
what magic is woven by
number seven

A Clarity Pyramid Chain of Love, Hate And Care

1
LOVE
passion
affection

promise to live life
together   forever
in sadness joy and danger

'love means not to say sorry ever.'

2.
HATE
dislike
abhorrence

shy away from love
build up   animosity
develop   antipathy

'not to stand each other anymore.'

3.
CARE
worry
sympathy

looking after her
in distress hardship woe
out of love once dear to both

"I love her, hate—yet her support."

I Love You

<pre>
      L   B
       O   L
        V   O
         E O
          M
          S
</pre>

like a rose
laid in bed of dust
wind warmth water run
as blood in veins
transformed
mind
mingles soul
leaving nothing
love is
heart-shaped
hangs on your

<pre>
          c
          l
          e
          a
          v
          a
          g
          e
</pre>

Eternal Bliss

Love is—
mother's care for child,
sister's protective eyes,
your lips, heart, soul,
waiting for my return;
prayer I utter for you
to the Almighty,
love's wingless bird--
eternal bliss.

Guardian Angel

Your lullaby fills the air mother
in harmony
Jasmines from the garden
weaves a dream in my eyes
the cuckoos add their melody
and fables of the woods

while listening to the fables
the lullaby
incensed by the fragrance
the Guardian Angel
folds his wings
and falls asleep in my arms...

Catalyst

y
o
u
r
fragrance
travels to me
s e n s a t i o n
touch ignites feelings
quivering lips taste nectar
bring   passion   to heights
satin skin creates magic
unite without knowing
when we reach
h e a v e n
in unison

On The Pathway of Rumi

Once I felt
the passion within
saw the glimmer of love
burning for you my world
has changed I concentrate
in guarding the flame from
outside storm and gale
cradling you like
a baby
every day
I sing a new lullaby
pacify you keep you busy
arouse you to new heights
now I have
only one star in
my sky one river of
sacred water and you are my
only lover my vision has changed
my notion directed like a
race horse when will
you call me in your
outstretched arms
my love...

Parting

Too loud a sound -- airborne
you cannot hear
Too deep a pain -- anesthetized
you never feel
Passions too close with bottle of wine
make you sober
Only candles feel --suffer
throughout the night -- alone
The pain of partings—
their tears drip till the dawn...

Archive

Love came to me
when you left me, youth
blooming garden looked barren
winter breeze blew in summer too
the body has forgotten the taste of spring

I started cleaning my soul
with sixty years' old archived wine
the best available in my archaic cellar

the night followed, the dance began
fellow pilgrims joined together

yet the tunes didn't mingle
parallel roads never cross each other
as the throne was not ready for your coronation
you went back

I have to start
all over again to invite you
to reach your love...

Morning Raga

The wind of imagery set sail the love-ship
colors abound in sky, forests and flowers
drift my thoughts across sea to you, my love,
words fail me, afraid I took shelter under covers.

Spring touches the river beds, the bees smitten
await quivering the opening of the first petals
eager to touch the pollen, impregnate them
but alas! I live alone in my dark corners.

Who will enlighten me and lead me to you
in this hour of self-doubt like insects in flowers
alone I cry in wilderness, sick with love
guarding a candle of hope with burning flicker.

'Songs of the earth are never dead,' so do flowers never die
I will live with dim hope, someday you will come nearby.

Unmask

my thoughts fly to you
like a Spring-bird
trying to build a nest in your hair

my eyes search for solace
in your tangent eyes
wish to suck the warmth from your lips

my hands want to touch
the plum snow-blossoms, smell it,
taste it with quivering lips

the murmuring rivulet
holds magic weave dreams
I fall asleep in your arms

Lavender, Jasmine's cascading effect
arouse the man in midnight
love's flower blooms
you hold an amazing smile
on your moonlit face
and always unmask my motives...

My Love For You

clasped in arms
you shiver like aspen-leaves
unknown fear intense desire

your rose-lips quiver
like half-bloomed flowers

I stare in trance
as the grasp loosens
you disappear like a doe
leaving me spell-bound...

Compliant

As the weeping willows
carves inward at the advent of Spring
the branches of apple tree
bend downwards with rich harvest
so you have set upon my soul
pliant, my lover

I turn to look upward
beyond the horizon
the crimson moon reminds me
of your trailing eye-brows
staring at me like a bow

longing grows within me
beyond all control
you never know when unbuttoned
your dress has fallen to the floor
compliant, we seek for more...

Seven Seas

The falling dewdrops in winter morning
kiss the rose-petals and say—
"I love you"

The flowing river Seine
touches the banks of Paris with Eros, says—
"Je t'aime"

The Reine passes through Black Forest
cleanses the feet of the woods
"Ich liebe dich"

The bleeding bulls fight till the last
yet congratulate the matadors
"Te Amo"

The boatmen quietly sing
while fishing in the Ganges
"Ami Tomay Bhalobashi"

I kiss your deep blue eyes, luscious lips,
touch your evergreen hills
down to Garden of Roses
and whisper in your ears in trance
"Amo Te", 'Ti Amo"
My Love...

Making of A Masterpiece

my masterpiece is yet to come,
as I traverse through the realms
of arts, painting, sculptures, psalms;

your face is painted in colors bright,
by the young artist in quivering light-
where your eyes and lips pose delight;

sculptor has chiseled your features sharp,
in black and white and shades of dark-
a marvel in stone with amazing spark;

I never know how to withstand a chance
to arrest in words your piercing glance,
or give shape to your beauteous stance;

words desert me, imagery looks shy,
metaphors feel gloom before bright eye-
how to describe you without alluring lie;

I feel disheartened without a goal,
though I love you with heart and soul:
unable to express me with console;

but I am sure to complete my work,
before I die of decease, hunger of shark--
my masterpiece will leave it's mark.

In Search of New Words

feeling tired of worn-out words
tenacious sounds of high decibel:

I am in search of some words which have no sounds
like falling of the dew-drops from night sky
Autumn-leaves dropping from trees
footsteps of the passing time
descending of evening at day-end

our quiet love-making throughout night
falling stars from the evening sky and the wishes you made
a hidden desire to travel back in time

the spreading of smile
through wrinkled face of the old lady like ripples on waves
or the rolling down of tears
along-side cheeks of the hungry girl-child
I saw outside the Puja pandal

I cannot forget them withstand those sounds
I weep within unheard at dead of night
let me have new words like your new dresses
to express me--- my feelings...

Shining Yogi

he steps out of his Mercedes
moves to the dais
the crowd burst into applause
eagerly awaits for his sermon

glossy silvery skin sparkles
glistens the gold rings studded with diamonds
in the setting rays of the sun

at night hidden cameras
find out his amorous sojourn
as compared to yogi he is

Intelligence Bureau unearths
millions of dollars in Swiss Banks
shinning golds in vaults
all in the name of meditation

the curtain is raised
in morning news papers
'all that glitters is not gold'...

I Wish If...

If I were a sculptor
I would have chiseled your beauty
your sharp features on stone
like Michelangelo and placed it at city center
to be adored by one and all

if I were an artist
I would have painted your face on canvas
like Picasso that holds the inviting eyes
smile luscious lips and sharp nose
that exudes pride and passion

if I were a musician
I would have created a symphony
like Beethoven to overflow in the ether
and traverse all barriers of nations
to fill the hearts and souls of listeners

but I am a poor poet
who hides dreams within his heart
attuned to soul and depict a frame
to hold your picture never seen by others
fragile as mirror dew drops on lotus leaves

I wish I could have held in imagery
all the emotions amorous erotica
that surfaced in my dreams and yours
in captivating words and metaphors
and adore you with a garland of roses...

but alas! I am no Pablo Neruda
unable to write for you
"Twenty Love Poems and a Song of Despair"
to win your heart and soul
now and forever...

Unison (A Loop Poem)

kinetic love kindles spirit
spirit transforms to fusion
fusion with kisses emits electricity
electricity transcends to power
power soothes the heart
heart transmits message of love
love begets love romance
romance entwine two souls
souls mingle together in unison
unison achieve key to peace...

A Time To Depart

it is high time to lift the anchor
sail into the unknown ocean again,
in search of a new fresh dwelling
leaving behind this green terrain;

let the guards salute for last time,
this land never belonged to us;
let beat of retreat flow in the air--
flag come down when the sun sets;

I'm a voyager, we can start afresh
the children will be taken care of;
whatever wealth we amassed here-
will be adequate for a new take off;

we'll carry love of people with us,
the memory of happiness to us belongs;
leave the palace, collect your belongings
dear, let's move in the path of life along.

Happiness

I searched for you in abundance
could not find the footsteps
I looked for you in wilderness
returned alone with look askance

had been to the Himalayas
followed the priests as disciples
meditation cleansed my soul, mind
but you were not to be found

after prolonged pilgrimage
while on my way back home
I found solace in a cottage
in a cold night, food warm

I realized in utter amazement
happiness you dwell over there
where minds are free, love is freer
flowing stream with heart's content

where truth lies in our thoughts
actions deeds are in conformity
where hard words are never exchanged
respect to others brings unity ...

there is no alternate to happiness
neither is it the means nor end
in our journey from life to death
happiness alone can share and mend

Printed in the United States
By Bookmasters